SKIES WIDE OPEN

How to Teach Your Child to Dream Big and Love Learning

TIMOTHY M. HORN

Hypnoconsult Publishing
Manassas, VA
©2018

Erin Pittman, Editor

Legal Disclaimer

All information in this book is offered for the betterment of education. The reader uses the information given with the understanding they have access to the ideas and principles and must apply them for their children or themselves. The reader is fully responsible for the utilization of the material and no legal or implied contract exists. Just as the book encourages questioning and challenging of all ideas as your child grows, the reader accepts their responsibility in positively implementing the material within.

CONTENTS

Dedication

This book is dedicated to the best teacher any child ever had, my sister Patricia Ann Warner.

I miss my sister.

Receive more strategies and tips from the author by signing up at www.SkiesWide.com.

PREFACE

As a public and private school teacher for over 20 years, I devoted my time to teaching my students how to learn. By reigniting within my students the love of knowledge, I was preparing them for their life's journey.

During my time as a public-school teacher, I was also a hypnotist and instructor with the National Guild of Hypnotists for over 25 years. The use of the mind and improvement of people's ability to learn and utilize new information has always been my greatest desire.

Having retired from teaching a few years ago, I still receive invitations from students and former colleagues to speak to their classes and show them how to maximize their learning experiences in school. In the past few years, I've been invited to several banquets where previous students have named me as their most influential teacher.

As an educator, I instilled in my students the belief that to change their lives, they just needed to change their mindsets. Change can be a bit frightening. We begin to stagnate and stand still because we are afraid of what might be ahead.

Before going into teaching, I was an average student who sabotaged my own success for fear of failing. I had the ability to succeed, but forcing myself to learn the way I was taught was frustrating. In life, you either run towards what you want or away from what you hate. I had come to hate school and avoided anything that related to it. As I learned more about the mind and the way we learn, I made it my mission, as a teacher, to show students a different path.

Several of my former students have gone on to attend prestigious colleges and lead successful careers. While I was teaching in Front Royal, Virginia, a letter arrived from Auburn University discussing the success of one of my former students. He had mentioned me as his greatest teacher.

He completed his sophomore year with a 2.2 GPA. After taking my Language Arts class and reframing the way he viewed school, he made tremendous progress. By the time he graduated he had improved his GPA to over a 3.3 with weighted honors classes.

After showing him new educational techniques, he realized he was far more capable of learning then he had ever dreamed. Not only did he learn more easily, but he could also take the knowledge he acquired and make connections to other ideas and thoughts that had previously seemed alien to him.

His confidence soared, and he began to succeed in all aspects of his life after discovering his natural method of learning and applying it to school and the way he viewed the world around him. He is now the vice-president of a networking company.

As you can see, this program is not merely designed to allow young students to succeed in an academic setting; it was created to expose students to a mindset and view of the world that opens up their imaginations to possibilities they only dreamt of.

If, after fully applying these techniques for three months, you have not seen an improvement in your child's attitude and success in school, contact me and I will issue a full refund. Within those three months, you'll notice your child making connections to things they previously would've ignored. You will find them more excited about going to school and acquiring more knowledge. You'll see them become more curious and observant of the world around them, bringing them greater joy in their everyday activities.

INTRODUCTION

Each child has the ability to learn and succeed. Children who began the early grades with the promise of great success sometimes seem to fall by the wayside as the difficulty of the work and the expectations of the teachers change. If, as a parent, you look forward to the day your child comes home smiling and speaking joyously of all the things he or she has learned at school, you've chosen the right book.

From the beginning of our existence as human beings, we create within our own minds our worldview. The shaping of that comes from those around us. Parents play a vital role in exposing their child to the world they live in. As they do, this exposure can be seen as either inviting or off-putting. If a child sees the world as inviting, they will invest in discovering its mysteries. If they see it as off-putting, they will shy from it and look to be protected.

This book is essentially a series of ideas and words strung together with a solid approach to execute. You are the active participant who can introduce these ideas and concepts to your child, so they can prosper in their lives.

Just as children quickly and naturally pick up language from birth from their parents and those around them, so too do they absorb your approach to and view of the importance of education. A child surrounded by piles of books and magazines that have clearly been opened already has the stage set for his or her future. If you are frequently caught off guard when called to dinner because your mind was lost in a new novel, you will be modeling the behavior your child could well benefit from.

You may well ask why these things are truly important. In modern society, children are frequently judged by how well they do in school, and when their grades are lacking, it affects their self-esteem. They feel betrayed by their inability to succeed and are constantly searching for ways to dig themselves out from an academic hole they feel they have created. As the stress amplified by their perceived failure weighs on them and prevents them from finding the solutions to their own problems, they become caught in a self-defeating cycle. It is a classic Catch 22 situation, and understandably, as a parent you may sometimes feel out of your depth as you try to support them.

The good news is there is a way to break this cycle. The best way to eat an elephant is one bite at a time, and, in this book, you will find simple and easily applicable steps that will enable your child to look at school as an opportunity to increase their ability to learn. No longer will they look at material they are forced to master as a necessity to regurgitate on an assessment. They will view their lessons as part of the game to demonstrate how well they learn. Their minds will begin making connections between each lesson as they meticulously build the road to a successful and happy future.

The program outlined in this book is your opportunity to open up your child's mind and imagination to the incredible world that surrounds them. All you need to do is to take action and create patterns that will allow them to live happier and more fulfilled lives. To accomplish that task, you can teach them to avoid the barriers they could inadvertently construct for him/herself. Every new thought creates a foundation to build upon. If the foundation is on shifting ground, the ideas that follow become compromised. As the first and most important models for that foundation, you have a wonderful opportunity to solidify its base. This is the right moment to do just that.

The program is designed to create new neural pathways, new ways of thinking and new approaches to everyday activities. These ideas will allow your child to become more actively engaged in life and to fully take advantage of their own natural intellect. It offers a chapter-by-chapter guide to viewing different aspects of your child's school life throughout the phases, reimagining them and creating a more open, accessible and thoughtful mind. It is equally relevant for both the parents of younger and older children who may need new tools to face the challenges of school.

As you introduce new ideas to your child, you might think of yourself as helping install new upgraded software in your child's mind. This analogy is particularly apt when you consider we all have accepted information (malware) that has compromised our main processing unit — our brains.

The book opens with explanations of how to empower the learner in the younger child and moves on to doing the same for the older student. By understanding the basic concepts, you will be able to modify these lessons for the appropriate level at which your child is operating.

As you go through this book, you'll see examples of good teaching in everyday life as well as at school. Like any other experience in life, it is how you react to an event that determines its value. Throughout this book I will give you tools, games and exercises for your child to use as they go to and from school. These games are designed to make their educational experiences more useful and beneficial in the long run.

Education is a journey, not a destination. Today they can begin that journey.

Conscious Mind

Subconscious Mind

Notice the disproportionate size of the subconscious compared to the conscious mind

TRANSITION TIME

My editor made an interesting point about what should happen before this chapter. You have read the introduction to the book. That introduction was designed to prepare you for the material that will follow. Where you expect it to go will determine how open you are to learning the new material. As we learn, we make a non-evident transition to becoming a scholar. We have a general idea of what we are going to learn. That very general idea leaves a large opening that needs to be filled.

In a future chapter, we'll discuss a few memory techniques. These techniques begin with the understanding that you will learn and enjoy it. If you look at this book and decide you will work to find things that will fail, your mind will find things that support or create weaknesses within the book. If you look for the things that will enable you to instill in your child that love of education, you mind will find those things. You can consciously transition your mind to be an open fertile place for learning and teaching.

As you read this book and even discuss it with your child, you are modeling the learning techniques you want them to employ. So many of today's children struggle due to a chaotic, busy, modern life. In that rush, adults forget young children need time — endless hours of caring connection with significant adults. And they need even more endless hours being an explorer and an adventurer discovering how the world works in order to build a brain that allows them to grow into being an independent, capable, resilient, caring human being in adulthood.

As you go through the book, lend your own imagination to the task at hand. There is a wonderful concept called "The Magical If." There are no constraints on your imagination that are not self-imposed. As you read through the ideas and games described, consider using "The Magical If" and question how your educational experiences might have changed had your parents read this type of book when you were young.

Now you have the opportunity to do just that. Investing in your child with your precious time and your own ability to learn will pay far more dividends that anything you will find in a book. Open your mind now, and thank you for your attention.

Chapter One

BUILDING EXPECTANCY

If you are reading this book, you clearly have your child's best interests at heart. You may have concerns about ensuring that your child's educational voyage stays on track, or you may want to ensure that you instill within your child a solid foundation to build their life upon. If so, you've come to the right place.

As you work through this book you will:

- Learn how to create a vivid educational landscape for your child.

- Discover more about your child's personality, which in turn, will foster a closer, more enjoyable relationship.

- Create the foundation to enable the life-long learner within your child to emerge.

- Discover elements and aspects that can reverse negative feelings your child may already have developed about school and learning.

Creating an expectancy of positive change can move any student to appreciate and love learning more.

Your Role As Navigator in Your Child's Journey

Education is about building a context for all the knowledge and events in your life. Context is the foundational work for education. Each thought and idea must be measured and considered against previous thoughts and ideas. Consider the play The Miracle Worker, the character of Helen Keller is untethered as she goes through her family's home. Losing her sight and hearing at infancy, her foundation to perceive the world was minimal. As her teacher Annie Sullivan places her hand underneath a water pump and her hand feels the cold wet liquid, the letters for water are repeatedly signed into Helen's other hand. The connections between the feeling of the water and the letters formed in her hand created an active context and start to break through the barriers deafness and blindness had created. As those barriers fall, her hunger for understanding, context and knowledge to gain an understanding of the outer world move her to greater things.

You truly are your child's first creator of context, so take that responsibility seriously. You have had experiences in your past that have, less dramatically than Helen Keller, created the context that allows you to see, hear, feel and taste the world differently than others. Your child needs that teacher to create that positive context and you are the best candidate.

Children will mirror the behaviors and actions they are exposed to — so if children see that their parents are curious and interested in the world around them, they will indulge in the same curiosity. We are our children's first and most lasting educational models.

You are responsible for creating the environment where education is a natural and enjoyable process. Before a child enters a public or private school, their view of learning and understanding of education have been established. When they find joy in exploring different ideas, the times waiting at the bus stop are filled with the excitement of what the new day will bring. That is the fertile ground upon which they can build a limitless future.

With the correct environment, their expectations for success and enjoyment are more likely to be realized.

Learning to Read the Map

It is said that even the longest journey begins with a single step, and that is certainly true. Your child is embarking on a journey of education. The important question that needs to be asked at the start of this journey is, "Where is my child going?"

Before shouting out, "Harvard" or "Oxford," consider this for a moment: If you had answered Harvard or Oxford, you have chosen a path before your child has even looked at a map. The first few chapters of this book are designed to enable you to show your child how to prepare to read that map. The destination will come from examining that map, exploring its dimensions and choosing a path.

Your child's journey is clearly not to a geographic destination, but the way they are taught to approach new ideas will affect how they accept, shape and utilize them.

I will start with the premise that to educate, we must narrow a child's understanding of different things. As you define something, you naturally end up fitting it into a smaller box. While you examine all the positive aspects of an idea or object, you must also determine which boxes it will no longer fit into. Your child's journey is clearly not to a geographic destination, but the way they are taught to approach new ideas will affect how they accept, shape and utilize them.

The way we formulate and accept impressions and feelings creates our greater worldview. As your child learns, they determine how to do those formulations and how to apply them. Frequently, that means categorizing those ideas and feelings as positive or negative.

Let me demonstrate this idea more literally. I start out planning my journey/vacation with no limitations, just possibilities. On a vacation/journey I then pare down my possibilities with every choice I make.

Where is your child going? As they are educated, you want them to be exposed to as many possibilities of growth as possible.

I plan a trip to Nova Scotia. My view of the trip begins to become defined and finite. I will not be going to California, Europe or Asia.

The beaches of Nova Scotia are certainly perfect for my taste, but they do not appeal to people who want to surf. They do not include the opportunity to see Broadway-quality shows or pick pineapples from trees. If on my journey I want to be able to include Broadway shows and pineapples, Nova Scotia would be excluded.

In finalizing my destination as Nova Scotia, I have opened up the opportunity for many exciting things, while simultaneously eliminating the possibility of a myriad of different opportunities for growth, enjoyment and pleasure.

The musical scene has a definite violin, guitar and folk flavor. The sounds of Maritimes are unique and different from most other places on the earth. Bars on the weekends are filled with live music and Cape Breton Step Dancing.

Life in Nova Scotia is set at a slower pace, and that

meets the inhabitants' need for excitement, as the pace matches their surroundings. There are limitations for this journey, but things that can appeal as well.Where is your child going? As they are educated, you want them to be exposed to as many possibilities of growth as possible.

I have just described an area of the world I love. Despite the limitations I acknowledge exist there, it is a place that feels like home. I had been exposed to many ideas, thoughts and possibilities before coming to acknowledge the positive feelings I have for that area.

I cannot possibly expect anyone to feel the same way about Nova Scotia as I do. All the experiences of my life have created within me a way of understanding and appreciating that special world that is mine alone. It is likely related to childhood memories of holidays where I was exposed to foreign yet familiar cultures. Perhaps my initial trip to Nova Scotia with my wife also created impressions that have resonated on a level I cannot consciously perceive. All those ideas are possible and even probable, but I believe it is something more.

If you believe we as human beings are born with a blank slate or tabula rasa, then all that we learn and how we learn it shapes and affects our perception of the world around us. We are taught from infancy how to do that shaping. When a parent interacts with a child, they begin communicating how that shaping should be done. They create the tools for perception.

After those learning imprints were made, I was equipped to decide from my life's experiences which things would leave a positive impression and which others would not. I learned how to evaluate the experiences around me from my parents and other stimuli. Those lessons, when applied, brought me to my appreciation of Nova Scotia.

To reiterate, certainly my experiences as a child were not focused exclusively on a large island off the coast of New Brunswick.

My experiences were not focused on taking long trips around the edges of an island I had never seen. My experiences were not focused on appreciating the calm and tranquility of small *seafaring towns or spotting moose as they traverse hilly terrain with their calves. But the culmination of all my experiences combined with my preschool lesson on how to perceive and evaluate the world helped create my unique perspective of that place. Nova Scotia is now my second home and a place of revitalization and rejuvenation for me. When children have been told that they are smart and capable, they will approach school and life with the attitude that they are smart and capable (told).*

When they have been shown that they are smart and capable they become smart and capable (shown). When they are complimented on being smart and capable, it becomes part of their hard wiring (actively doing).

When children have been told that they are smart and capable, they will approach school and life with the attitude that they are smart and capable (told). When they have been shown that they are smart and capable they become smart and capable (shown). When they are complimented on being smart and capable, it becomes part of their hard wiring (actively doing).

You may be feeling comfortable and believe so far you have been doing a good job reinforcing an open mind in your child. Consider this though: The context you create as you do that reinforcement is crucial.

Preparing for that Journey

How do we prepare a child for the journey that is about to begin with an undefined destination? How can we make this journey one that will create reference material to judge their life's experiences against? When a child starts with the ability to use all the stimuli around them in a positive way, they have gained a wonderful perspective. The culmination of the stimuli creates the map-reading ability for all future knowledge. Perhaps it would be an appropriate paradigm shift.

If a child has limited defined experiences, the world could paradoxically offer so much more. They've not been told the limitations of the world that exists. Clearly the idea is not to produce children who expect the world to be perfect; however, if children are open from the start to all the possibilities and ways of viewing the world, the world becomes a place of openness and opportunity.

Allow your children to view life as it appears to them. Shape, but do not diminish, how they view that life.

My natural curiosity, which was fostered from the time I was a child, exposed me to worlds of which I had no first-hand knowledge. Imprints and impressions were accepted and started to create my greater worldview. I accepted the things around me and attempted to put them into the right kind of context. The context in this case was that of a young boy interested in the world, not just Nova Scotia.

As a young child, the greatest lesson I learned was the power of questions. Trying to find the answers to questions forced me to think more deeply about the world around me. It was not as important to know something as it was to know where I could find information to guide me.

Libraries supplied that information; there is no question of that, but realizing and forming questions to ask were equally important and fed by my undying curiosity. In truth, forming questions in a positive way that demonstrates a burgeoning curiosity in a subject or area of interest is a clear indicator of a fertile mind.

We all start with that natural curiosity. Everything has a newness and surprise as we start out. From birth, we are attempting to find our place in the world. Things that are new have to be placed in our expanding perception. When this new information comes in early on, being open-minded benefits the child, but its difference from previous experiences can be strange. The very nature of new information is the problem of finding its relevance without an understanding based on previous knowledge. As open-mindedness is honored and praised, the natural inquisitive nature of a child overcomes the slight discomfort they may feel as they stretch their minds to understand unfamiliar information.

When I asked a question, my mother would compliment my inquisitive nature, and then together we would begin to explore possible answers. At the basic level, this created within me the desire to ask questions and to appreciate the joy of the hunt and discovery of answers. My mother seemed to revel in my desire to learn and the need to please her pushed me to continue. My questioning nature was complimented and honored. Had I perceived resistance to answering the questions or spending time exploring for answers, my curiosity may well have been affected in a negative way.

The fact that she did not merely give me a direct and limiting answer allowed me to create my own personal, and less limited, context from which to view the world. As I look back, I realize that part of the excitement of searching for answers was the idea I could help my mother in her confusion. My mother was a brilliant woman who clearly did not need to take as much time researching the topics we did. Her joy was in seeing her son learn at a foundational level the excitement of self-education.

When a parent merely gives a child an answer without allowing them to explore, they prevent them from having the joy of the journey that culminates in arriving at their own special destination. Beyond that, it can even indirectly downplay the search for knowledge.

Education has greatly shifted in the past thirty years. Computers now make the search for knowledge a few clicks away. No longer is a trip to a public or even a private library necessary. This could well downplay the importance of the knowledge itself. We tend to value more the things we have had to fight or work for.

Sometimes it is not the answer that is most important but being able to ask the right question. Honor the questions your children ask; they will show you how they are thinking.

As a young student, there was no definitive destination as my journey began. There was no map assigned to me to achieve happiness in my adult life. There was an open, undefined world from birth that I was left to discover and categorize for myself with help from parents, family and close friends. I was no different from anyone else on that count, and certainly no different from an average student.

The advantage I had over many students was that my parents respected the questions I asked them and seemed genuinely interested from where they came. A mutual trust developed that lasted through my school career. My interactions with my parents were my earliest schooling as they modeled what a good teacher would be. My parents were less interested in demonstrating their own intelligence to me than they were in finding out about mine.

As I went to school, I met many excellent teachers. Unfortunately, I also met many teachers who did not match the model my parents had shown me. These teachers were undoubtedly well-meaning and concerned with their students; however, they were also concerned with meeting their obligation to the school board and parents.

Equipping Your Child for the Road

We must acknowledge from the very beginning that no child lives a perfect life. Adversity rears its ugly head at every turn. When difficulties come up in children's lives, being smart and capable will enable them to deal with and overcome those challenges more adequately. The initial shock of the difficulties can be exacerbated by a parent who overreacts and creates a deeper negative imprint from the incident. Using early difficulties as an opportunity to demonstrate coping skills changes the paradigm of the issue itself.

If a young child falls to the ground and scrapes his knee or hands, complimenting them as they get up and are telling them they are strong while sympathizing with the initial physical discomfort highlights the importance of resilience as obstacles arise. Running to the child in a frightened and distressed state could increase the damage done from the simple event.

Applying their minds to those problems creates context for their lives. Problems contextually become opportunities to use what they know and how they react to these difficulties. After learning and applying the information in a positive way, the context will be "learning makes life easier and more enjoyable." The more adaptable and capable you are, the easier it is to deal with the everyday vagaries of life.

Living life in fear of making mistakes is a losing proposition.

As they will be viewing the obstacles that occur in life as commonplace and normal, those challenges become the metal to test their abilities against. The word or concept of normal actually is an important one.

Normal is everyday and expected. Its energy is even and not off-putting. Normal occurs and then is dealt with without much of a second thought. There is no additional pressure of dealing with the unknown or unexpected. The negative impact of the unexpected, which can cause a tightening or imbalance, is non-existent. This allows the natural self-correcting nature we are born with to come forward.

When children see new difficulties as commonplace, they begin to expect to deal with them more easily. What is expected tends to be realized.

If they go to school and have been told from the very beginning to be careful not to make mistakes or to make certain they get along with everyone, their caution may prevent them from achieving a full educational experience. If, however, their understanding of life includes the realization that mistakes will be made, they can engage in all the learning opportunities more freely. Their fear of making mistakes is superseded by the joy of overcoming mistakes to ensure they do not reoccur.

When a child returns from school, don't be afraid to call their attention to mistakes to show them the benefit of how they can lead to positive life lessons. Repeated habits become part of the deep hardwiring that lasts. If you ask your child what mistake they made in school that day, it could sound like an attempt to find fault, but it can become instructive when the query is combined with a follow up question that directs them to a lesson.

After getting a general sense of their day and praising them for the good they have done, you can address any issues. Don't skip this part. It's important. "What do you think you did wrong in class today?" Discuss the problem in a calm, open, logical manner. Don't draw it out, nag or escalate the emotions.

"Okay, and what are you going to do to make sure that you will not repeat the mistake?"

By asking your child this question every day, you show them you do not expect perfection, but improvement. Beyond that, you show them that when they are honest in evaluating their mistakes, the consequences will be minimal. Every day this question comes up, your child will begin to see you as a partner in their growth. By sharing the slightly painful events that occur, your child will learn to trust you even when things are not going smoothly.

When greater issues come up and your child truly needs to confide in you, you will have established a positive open model. Coming to you with difficulties and for advice in dealing with them will be commonplace and simple. As they age, those patterns will remain even when difficult questions that plague middle and high school students arise.

The day may come when your child has had an outstanding day and they feel like nothing that went wrong was truly noteworthy. Those days would be wonderful, but the other days could actually be of greater benefit. It's all in how we perceive the events and what we do to maximize the lessons we learn from them.

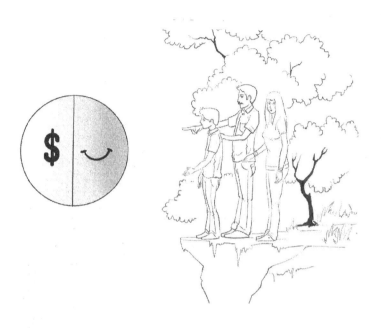

Stepping Up After Falling Down

After graduating from college, I had the opportunity to work at a Living History gathering in St. Mary's, Maryland. One of the more enjoyable aspects of the experience was meeting jugglers and other entertainers. I would never become nearly as proficient as they were, but I did learn how to juggle at a basic level.

The first lesson I learned was that I would drop the objects I was juggling. Sometimes I would throw them out too far. Sometimes I would throw them too close. Each time I practiced, I became more proficient. The fear of making a mistake soon disappeared, and the natural rhythmic patterns for juggling became ingrained. Fear serves a purpose as a guide for protection; however, when we are overprotective, fear becomes disabling and we cannot move forward.

This was a valuable lesson for a 24-year-old. Looking back at that time, I realized that lesson could have been taught to me much earlier on and, from an early age, prevented me from struggling with the fear of failure.

If I had been told from the very beginning that life includes the benefit of dropping the ball and picking it up again, that negative charge that coursed through my body when I dropped the ball would have been lessened. If children live their lives in fear of making mistakes, they may choose not to venture the attempt. The only people who never fail are people who do nothing.

If our kids live their lives understanding that the fear of failure stops them from moving forward, they cannot help but progress. In those open fields in St. Mary's, the experience of learning was tied in to the joy of working with a company of professional actors and entertainers who loved what they did. That is the optimal environment for learning.

As they say, the master has failed more times that the student has tried.

You will fail. Failure is not a mistake until you decide not to learn from it.

In my juggling analogy, my teachers' joy in what they did certainly helped.

The human equation in that learning process cannot be discounted. When a child goes to school, that same human equation will be different, yet similar. The interactions children have are fraught with the opportunity of both failure and success.

Exposure

I would suggest that one of the most important aspects of school life is forming friendships with people who are different. You might consider this exploring the unknown at the personal level.

Each child or teacher your child meets creates a new experience to evaluate and qualify. These evaluations are far more fluid than pictures or words in a book. The diversity of each individual offers opportunities for growth far different from what you have read or shared with your child.

New people are the ultimate unknown, and that can be a frightening or exciting thing for your child. As mentioned before, things that are new represent a step away from the normal. New friends and teachers may well represent as Shakespeare said, "the undiscovered country." This country may well be different and strange. Those descriptions do not preclude that great benefits can come from exploring these new realms of human relationship.

Children should be encouraged to form friendships with others who may be culturally different and of a different age. Without your positive encouragement, they may pass on the opportunity these new relationships offer.

How children react to the people around them when they enter school will determine what type of environment they create for learning. This is based on their experiences with family and friends even before they walk through their first school hall.

People, unlike books, evolve, change and adapt to the world around them. Your child must understand that the people he/she comes into contact with are going through the same growth and learning process they are. As they learn to appreciate the difficulties and excitement of their own development, they will begin to see it in the people they encounter in school as well. When your child sees and recognizes their own movement to growth, they will be able to appreciate it in others. The more different groups of people your child experiences, the stronger their ability to differentiate between individuals and culture becomes.

There is an important distinction between evaluating and judging. While a child can have an understanding of the actions of another person, it may still cause them to be uncomfortable and avoid them. The importance of understanding why they wish to avoid the child can prevent escalated confrontations in the future. Boundaries are an important element in life.

Teaching a child appropriate boundaries for themselves and others is very important. These early lessons establish the foundations for all their future interactions. But those lessons need to be taught in a way that is instructive, firm, and yet, non-threatening. They must not associate the learning of boundaries with pain or discomfort.

Understanding that consequences are not punitive, but instructional, begins at home.

It has been widely reported that the first word children learn is "no," and that in and of itself is an indictment of our approach to learning. Perhaps a good learning analogy would be the experience all children go through in their early years. When a child is young and their parents watch them walking toward a burner, the natural impulse is to protect the child. This protection frequently comes with a loud shout that leaves a negative impression with the child. What you are teaching the child to do is to avoid being caught or yelled at.

An alternative way to teach the child to avoid the danger is to expose them to a small amount of it. As a child gets closer and begins to feel the heat, they learn the lesson while utilizing all their senses. The lesson is not experienced simply by hearing the word no, but by the child feeling the heat and responding naturally for self-protection. As they feel that heat and the self-protective instinct appears, discuss it with them. This is the natural way of learning. The gentle warning combined with the discomfort of heat imbeds the context of living your life safely without stifling the desire to explore outside constricting comfort zones. The lessons learned this way are engrained at multiple levels of the mind maximizing their effectiveness.

This does not mean I am advocating exposing children to danger at every turn, but being overprotective can stifle growth. If they perceive danger around every corner, they will never leave the house.

In the same way, parents frequently try to prevent their children from playing in the dirt and mud. When children are not exposed to the normal pollens and dirt particles, their immune systems have nothing to utilize to develop a resistance, and their bodies are incapable of fighting off these everyday hazards.

As parents, our best intentions do not always lead

to the best results. Brief exposures to different stimuli, such as dirt, allow children to adapt, modify and learn coping behaviors biologically and behaviorally.

By allowing your child to run a small errand, to deliver something to a neighbor, to count out money and pay for something in a shop, you are exposing them to everyday situations they will learn to cope with. When your child walks to school for the first time, they will have expectations of new experiences and will have developed the tools to adapt, learn and utilize what those experiences have brought.

Like any other lesson, if they do not have the tools, frustration will set in. When frustration arises, the natural reaction is to shut down. Expose your child to new experiences and keep monitoring and shaping their reactions. It will result in a more confident, capable child. This will pay long-term dividends as they embark on their journey of education.

Teach your children to live their life with caution, but not fear.

Let the World Be Your School

All education must be student-based. This should be a universal truth. Because education systems the world over do not have as their basis the best way for children to learn, it is crucial for you as a parent to recognize and step into this gap.

It is assumed that as children enter school, they have come supplied with their own learning tools. Their education will occur within their minds. Books, teachers and other ancillary things are just tools to get into those minds.

Children must be encouraged to create within themselves the ability to take their lessons in and out of school and to manipulate them to their own way of thinking.

This will enable your child to take experiences and place them into a personal context that is familiar and accessible to them as holistically as possible.

Children will learn from teachers with varying styles and methods. Creating within them the joy of questioning and learning will push them forward to adapt to all teaching methods.

The following game is designed to give your child the opportunity to speculate and to consider possibilities they had never considered before. There are no wrong answers, and the questions should be intentionally open-ended. Your role is to honor the imagination of your child and not to correct them. Allow the game to develop into an opportunity for further learning by saying, "It's a very interesting thought. We will have to look into that."

This game can be pitched at different levels appropriate to your child's age. Some examples are shown below, but attempt to produce your own.

Game One
If You Knew...

This first question is for a child who is starting school, kindergarten or first grade.

Show your child pictures of a man walking on the moon. After doing this, ask them: "If you knew how we got on the moon, how would you explain it to me?"

One of the first and most important steps in learning is to realize you do not need to be right the first time. By asking the child a question you know they cannot answer fully, you are allowing them the opportunity to speculate and consider possibilities they had never considered before. The way the question is formed precludes the possibility of not knowing an answer.

Whatever they say, tell them, "It's a very interesting thought. We will have to look into that." This allows a child's imagination to be honored. By not shutting down or correcting the child at this point you give them the opportunity to speculate and consider possible answers. You also explained to them that after they come up with an idea they should examine whether it is correct or not.

Some additional *If You Knew...* game questions:

Show them a picture of a child from another country and ask, "If you knew what his/her life was like, how would you describe it?" When they are done, compliment them and ask how they came up with their ideas.

Each time you participate in this sort of game, you empower your child to be unafraid of going out on a limb and making guesses. When you follow up with questioning why, you begin to fine-tune their reasoning abilities. Their ability to weed out less likely scenarios increases as they take in more information. The definitions created narrow possibilities down.

Some of the things they may notice in the picture are the scenery, animals, clothing or the style of the houses. They are informing you on how they make judgements and assessments of the world around them. Be supportive and discuss their ideas with them.

You need not only rely on pictures. If you see your child getting excited about any event, match their excitement and say, "This is so great! Tell me what you like so much about it."

Each event you discuss will create new neuropathways for your child and allow them to make greater and more frequent connections to the people and events that surround them. This is the creation of context done at the organic level.

These questions are focused on children just as they are beginning school, because when children are young, they take in the information and are more easily influenced. But by logically modifying and working with your middle school or even high school students, the process remains the same.

If You Knew... questions for older children:

If you have a middle-school child, this next question would be more appropriate. They will have begun to see how things are interconnected and the following type of question will reinforce their knowledge of that interconnection.

Ask your child this question:"If you understood absolutely everything related to a light bulb and the way it is used or created, what would you know?"

As you listen carefully to your child's answer, think about this: The question is intentionally open-ended.

How would you answer that question? Would you consider only the light bulb itself and its components?

Would you consider the materials used to create it?

Would you consider the fact that most light bulbs include a vacuum, and if they understood vacuums they could understand space?

Would you consider the effect the light bulbs caused on the economy?

Edison had to create electrical grids to feed electricity into the homes. His designs were faulty and brought about the argument between direct and alternating current. If you understood absolutely everything related to the light bulb, you have to understand optics and all that it encompasses. You have to understand how light has mass and can be sucked into a black hole. You have to understand the effect changing from open flames to electrical lighting had on fire departments. Some of these concepts, i.e. optics and how current flows, may be foreign to you. Were you to have a passion for the topic, you would explore all its aspects.

All these things are related to understanding one single object. If your child understood all the elements connected to the creation and the use of the light bulb and all it does, they would understand the universe.

When your child shows a passion for a topic, they are showing their gateway to learning. As you feed that passion and the hunger for more information increases, they will begin to see the interconnections that create a fuller understanding of the topic.

If children understand the interactions and overlapping of all the things around them, they create a greater context for their education. This principle applies to elementary, high school and college students.

If You Knew... follow-up questions:

When a child loses their fear of being wrong, every attempt to expand their knowledge base becomes an educational opportunity.

Periodically ask similar questions to your child. Being supportive and enjoying the exchange of ideas is the key to this exercise.

Other questions to ask include:

If World War II had not been fought, how would the world be different today?

If you could erase one major figure from history, who would it be and how would they have affected the way the world developed?

If you had to choose one quality that every friend of yours must have, what would that be? What quality is totally unacceptable for your friend and why?

It is in this way that a child understands the interactions and overlapping of all the things around them and, unknowingly, how they create a greater context and model for their own education.

Make this a fun activity and incorporate it into your long drives in the car or your long winter evenings. Be creative and use the elements around you. Point out the stars, the garden or even the cash register when you are stuck in a long queue in a supermarket. Being supportive and enjoying the exchange of ideas is the key to this exercise.

As children start learning, it is better for them to give you too much information and to pare down the answer from there. This gives them the courage to put themselves on the line without fear of failing.

In life we run towards what we love or away from what are afraid of. When a child loves the positive reinforcement they get when they ask questions, they will continue to do so. If a child is afraid to ask questions, they will merely stop engaging. Continue to nurture and encourage the inquiring mind of your child.

Practice does not make perfect. Practice makes permanent. Practice this exercise frequently with your child with the idea that when they are "wrong," they deserve to feel good for making the attempt. Let them know that their point of view is interesting and worth examining.

Asking them questions to lead them to better ideas shows them how to formulate and challenge new thoughts. When they have this sort of interchange in the safe environment of their home, they'll be much more willing to open up in school. Indeed, when the time comes to examine their ideas and modify them, they will have experienced the joy of growth and discovery that was created organically.

The Classroom

If your child enters school with the expectation of exploring their new experience for answers, they become fully prepared for school itself. They will begin to realize all their life's experiences teach them something of value. Your child's expectations of being able to think and enjoying the active learning experience are the fertile grounds upon which their lives are built.

We have not gotten to the school section of the book yet, but this will become an important question, so we will raise it now.

At this point, you may be wondering how to navigate external forces that have an influence on your child.

As part of your evening routine, or while sitting around the dinner table, ask your child what they learned that day. Try to be specific and ask what was taught in a certain subject so they do not engage with you vaguely.

If their learning experiences have been positive to that point, they should be able to identify the way in which they learn best, even though they may be exposed to a different teaching approach at school. Simply ask them, "If the teacher taught you in the best way possible for you to learn, how would they have done that?" This question will engage your child's mind in a creative way and cause them to actively examine their lessons for the day.

Here's an example of how one student put this into practice. I recently spoke to a mother whose high school son was an excellent student, but who was having difficulty with his science class. The teacher would merely put up PowerPoint slides for him to copy.

He knew that he loved music, so he decided to write songs that covered the material in an interesting way. This approach caused him to become engaged while in class, as well as when he came home. As the teacher taught, he was already modifying the lesson to his best method of learning.

Television

When children are younger, they take in everything and are easily susceptible to influence. If they watch television, ensure the shows they watch create and support a questioning nature.

If they watch shows that are clean and complete in 30 or 60 minutes and do the thinking and exploring for them, they become passive learners. By their nature, television shows frequently present an issue to be dealt with and the accompanying complications that prevent it from being handled easily. This causes the conflict, which draws in an audience's attention. The protagonist or main character of the show then overcomes the issue in some way to leave a solid understandable resolution. For example, the criminal confesses and justice is established for the populace of the town. Perhaps a character has discovered that lying to their parents is not right and they have grown.

Children will normally be exposed to television that is simpler, and, as they age, the material becomes more complex. It is important to let children know that life is not always clean or neat. Additionally, problems are not normally resolved in an hour or less.

To learn fully, we must engage the mind actively by questioning. Watching television with your child and discussing the shows will create a more active learner.

Be open to letting your children discover things
without placing heavy-handed judgements on them.
They are creating their own world within their
minds, and you are helping them to have a positive
feeling about it.

Chapter Two

PERSPECTIVE

Everything your child learns and how they learn will leave a long-term impression upon them and will be instrumental in shaping their educational journey. The foundations for a holistic educational journey are rooted in a questioning nature.

From a child's perspective, there will always be questions that need to be answered. The way you, as a parent, answer these questions is vitally important as well. Every question you answer helps them understand the educational process.

One of the most existential questions is: "Why am I here?" Every time you talk to a child in one way or another, you are, in fact, answering this question for them. If a child asks you a question that they perceive engages you, their purpose on earth will be to keep you engaged.

From the very beginning, children are taught by those around them what their place in the world is. If you show them love and respect, they will feel loved and respected. As mentioned in the first chapter, this does not mean that a child should live without boundaries; however, when the boundaries and their purpose are explained with the implication that the child will understand and respect them, then the child will do just that.

Your expectation of your child will tend to be realized. Let them know what your expectations are. For example, you may expect that your child will run into obstacles that make life more challenging and they will face them fearlessly and share them with you. In terms of learning, those expectations might be that they will learn easily, enjoy the experience of learning and want more. When their expectation of the world coincides with those ideas, their fear of going into the world and learning is eliminated.

It is important for a child to have a self-perspective of being capable, intelligent and interested. Building a child's own self-image to be positive and productive creates the intellectual environment to realize those two states. This does not mean your child is incapable of making errors; however, the way you deal with mistakes will determine whether they are viewed as a learning experience or as a punishment.

As mentioned earlier, how we fall and get up is important. We inadvertently implant negative feelings within our children without realizing it. As human beings, we tend to be self-correcting. You undoubtedly have seen a child fall on the ground and get up looking around to see if anyone noticed. The little one seems fine, relatively happy, but maybe a little surprised that they have fallen.

This all changes when the parent runs up screaming, "Are you all right? Are you all right?" Invariably the child ends up crying and what should have been a simple experience of falling down and getting back up again has now been turned into a negative episode in their life.

That simple impression remains with them for the rest of their lives. Had smiling parents approached the child talking about how happy they were that he had gotten up again, they would have reframed the entire episode. The focus would be on the fact that the parents were proud of the child falling and being able to get up. That is truly more than a simple metaphor.

Children will fall. Children will not always meet expectations. While these two things are to be expected, the fact that they can learn from their failures and move on positively, is not. If a child has enough self-confidence to take the negative experiences and learn from them, they can release the pain, the stress and the anxiety they might have retained from those negative experiences.

There is nothing either good or evil, but thinking makes it so.
–Adapted from Shakespeare

How you react to an event affects how clear your child's memory and perception of that event will be. Your purposeful response to the child falling could well move them from fear to the feeling of resilience as they get up.

When I was teaching high school English, one of my greatest frustrations occurred during the opening day of school. I would ask my students what they expected to learn from my class. Without fail, half the class would tell me about how horrible they were in English. They would regale me with stories of how they had failed miserably in the previous classes, how they couldn't spell, how they didn't know an adjective from an aardvark.

Some of these feelings were created in their previous class when they were incapable of warding off their negative experiences with their teachers or the subject.

The first two weeks of class would be used to build up my students so that they realized that they were smart and capable. Each one of those children had knowledge that I had never been exposed to. Many were from different cultures, spoke different languages and had traveled to places I had never heard of. Yet they were incapable of acknowledging their ability to learn and share what they had.

The past may be prelude, but the lessons you learn do not have to be negative.

There were two Buddhist monks, an older master and his student walking along a river stream contemplating the beauty of the day and all nature had to offer them. They came upon a young woman who seemed in distress. The stream was narrow at that point and she needed to cross it. Despite the fact the river was shallow, her fear of drowning prevented her from crossing on her own. These two monks had taken vows not to touch women, yet the old master lifted her and carefully carried her across the narrow river, safely depositing her on the other side and returned to his student's side.

The two monks walked silently for the next day and a half, camping at night and enjoying a simple meal and the wonders of nature that surrounded them. Despite the tranquility, it was clear the young monk was preoccupied with the actions of his wise master. On the second day, he finally asked, "Master, we took a vow not to touch women, yet two days ago you carried that woman across the river and dropped her on the other side. Why did you do that?"

The old master smiled and said, "Yes, two days ago I dropped that woman on the other side, but for the past two days you have continued to carry her."

My students carried the failures of the past when they served no purpose in educating them. All they needed to keep were the lessons the failures taught them, not the failures themselves.

This negativity would also affect the positive students

in my class. They sometimes would feel like outsiders who were different because they were smart. As children we naturally want to fit in. When being smart prevents your child from fitting in, he may try to fit in by not doing his best.

Different is not always bad.

No child learns in exactly the same way, and not all children will be geniuses. However, each child has the potential to learn a great deal more than they allow themselves to. Our aim is to release the learner within your child.

Parallels with Hypnosis

In my over 25 years as a hypnotist, one of the questions I frequently ask my clients is whether or not they feel they deserved to be happy. You would be truly amazed at how many people say no. For whatever reason, they have accepted the lies and misperceptions thrust upon them by others.

Part of this is a learned point of view. When a child is young and someone corrects them, it is vitally important that from the very beginning the child realizes that every correction is filled with a lesson for them to learn. It is every parent's desire for their child to view life in the most positive way possible. To do this, they will try to emphasize the importance of not making mistakes along the way. To put greater emphasis and more importance on these corrections, parents will frequently raise their voices, shout or become emotional negatively affecting the child's learning experience.

In the previous chapter, we discussed imprints that are made when a child falls. The words and tone used when correcting a child can cause damage or build confidence.

Either one can set a precedent that carries on throughout the rest of their lives. This is where perspective truly comes into play.

One of the most frequent issues I have to deal with as a mind coach is attempting to mend relationships within families. A mother may be telling her 14-year-old son that he has to be home by 7 o'clock and to let her know where he is. From a parent's perspective, this is an act of love and protection. A 14-year-old attempting to create his own identity in that situation may well view it as an attack on his freedom or a lack of trust. The same action is viewed in two entirely different ways. Teaching a child to view events through different perspectives is very beneficial.

It is vitally important from the very beginning that a child learn that when corrections are being made, the intention is positive, not punitive.

When a child goes to school with the created understanding that a correction means they've done something wrong and deserve punishment, learning becomes substantially harder. If, early on, a child understands that when they're corrected it is done out of concern with the intention of them moving forward in a positive manner, a solid foundation is established. When a teacher corrects them, they can view the correction as it was intended. The imprint of the possibility of positive change has been created. The correction becomes an opportunity for growth, not humiliation.

There is an enormous difference between what is intended and what is perceived.

Feed the Passion

Another important aspect of a child's growth is

feeding their passion for whatever interests them. We touched on passion earlier, and this concept needs to be expanded upon. When I was young, many things we discussed and read in class were not interesting to me. In second and third grade, my reading was always competent and on a level with everyone else. There was nothing exceptional in my learning, other than my great curiosity for the things around me.

There was one thing that truly drew my interest. I loved baseball. Every Saturday, I would sit down and watch a game. I would overhear the announcers talk about batting averages and earned run averages (ERA). They would go into great detail about previous baseball players who had done incredible things. This just fed my interest.

Because of this passion, I decided to read as many biographies of baseball players as I could, and the reading level of many of these books was slightly higher than my grade level. This caused me to improve my reading to feed the passion that was within me. I perceived my reading as a way to better understand the game I loved.

My mathematics grades had been fair, and my teachers felt I showed a great aptitude in it, but the final push to truly delve into the numbers involved my love of baseball. I soon learned how to divide, add and subtract so I could keep up with the batting averages of all the players on the field. (Slightly more difficult was figuring out a pitcher's ERA.)

By feeding that passion, I began to see mathematics as a useful tool to increase my enjoyment of the sport I loved. As I became fully engulfed in this passion, I decided to examine the history of baseball, which led me to learn about the effects of not only the World Wars on the game, but also racism.

In the books I read, people went to the wars and died. Their lives ended. Pictures and discussions of people I had no connection to were covered page after page. Those pages explained in detail the loss of life in a clear and concise manner, but when I learned about the exploits of Christy Mathewson, one of the greatest pitchers of the early 20th century, the loss became less clinical.

After investing my passion for baseball in reading his autobiography, I discovered that Mathewson, a non-smoker and health enthusiast, lost his life to pneumonia because of the effects of a training accident during World War I. World War I had a more personal and lasting context for me after learning of his fate. To me, he exemplified what a baseball player should be at the league's inception, and yet he was unable to avoid the horrors of war.

Jackie Robinson broke the color line in Major League Baseball in 1947, but in reading his biography, I discovered he had been an officer in World War II who had nearly been court-martialed for refusing to give up his seat on a bus near his military base. He stood his ground and was exonerated. This added to his experiences as a Brooklyn Dodger in 1947 and gave me a larger understanding of the sociology of race in America before I was born.

Reading, mathematics, history and sociology were introduced to me through my one true passion as a child — baseball. This education developed organically.

If your child has a passion and you encourage it, that passion can become a road to education. Aiming your child towards these sorts of discoveries and using their passion does take a bit of creativity, but it is well worth the effort.

In doing so, you acknowledge their passion and reinforce it within them. You open up lines of communication while showing additional interest in what they're doing. You create a common language between child and parent that can allow the lines of communication to remain open.

Learning Methods Game

Educators have broken down the way children learn into several modalities, which simply refers to categorizing which methods they use to learn best. In the following game, you will be asking your child to engage their imagination. Education is primarily a creation of the imagination taking information and placing it where it will be accessible in the future.

To use this technique, I recommend reading over the following story to yourself several times until you become fairly comfortable with it and are able to allow your voice to express some of the emotions and tensions that might be present.

This exercise is designed to see what type of learner your child may be. This is not definitive, but it could provide you a better grasp on how to approach your child when discussing homework or anything else.

Game Two — Making Lemonade

Let's play a game using your imagination. Sit down for a moment and listen carefully to this story. Close your eyes.

I want you to imagine coming in from the hot, muggy outside into the kitchen. Because it was so hot outside, you could imagine coming in barefoot feeling the cold floor against your feet. Having been outside in the heat for so long you might be able to feel that thirst building up inside you. You slowly move toward the refrigerator and take your time as you're so drained from being outside in the heat for so long.

Reach out to the refrigerator and begin to pull it open. You may hear the seal crack as the door swings open. Feel the cool air from the refrigerator come out as you look in and see a bright, beautiful lemon on a plate. You take the plate out and put it on the counter as you reach to get a nice sharp knife and prepare to cut the lemon.

Feel the lemon with all its light indentations in your hand as you place it down either on the plate or the cutting board, whichever you prefer. You take the knife and begin to slowly cut into it lengthwise. As you cut you can feel the fibers within the lemon begin to give way to the sharp blade. You can feel the juice of the lemon squirting through its skin, filling the air with a lemon scent. The juice of the lemon covers your hand making it just a little bit sticky. The knife finally comes through and clanks against the plate or cutting board.

You lift the lemon up and begin to smell it, so fresh and clean. You begin to cut the half lemon one more time down the middle, feeling more of the juice cover your hand and pour onto the plate.

You take this remaining piece of lemon and bring it slowly up to your mouth. You might be able to smell the freshness but are careful that none of the juice squirts into your eye. Open your mouth and put the lemon slice into it, biting down, as you suck the juice out of it.

After completing the story, ask your child if they could feel the cold on their feet as they walked on the floor, if they could hear the refrigerator crack open, if they could feel the lemon give way as they cut into it, if they could smell the fresh lemon or feel it on their hand. Finally, ask them if they could taste the lemon as they bit on it.

There are multiple ways in which children learn. Some learn by listening, some learn by seeing, some by touching and some learn by smelling. This story will show you which sense is strongest for your child. When the child understands their best method of learning, they have the tools to take whatever lessons come their way and modify them so that they can learn in the best way possible.

Earlier I discussed a student who loved music, so he took the lesson his science teacher taught him and turned it into a song. He was an auditory learner.

Some students are **visual** learners and others **tactile**.

How can a teacher possibly approach and teach all these different modalities? Some teachers are capable of doing this, but many are unable to. It is our duty to enable our children and to help them identify what works for them and how to best adapt.

Visual learner: Creating a storyboard for the information could do wonders if your child seems to be a visual learner. Imagining a movie with images that explores the theme and emphasizes what the teacher has stressed could help to cement the images in their minds. The subject does not matter, and this can apply to science as well as language arts and history. With practice, they can create a visual story that closely matches what they will need to retain. No matter what the subject, pictures and images could be created and associated with the material studied.

Tactile learner: A similar approach can be applied to the tactile learner. Creating a diorama or topographical map for the story that is written could well help them take in and absorb the material. Creating models for the elements they are studying can give them the feel of the material they are studying. These are just a few of the techniques that a tactile, hands-on, learner can benefit from.

When a teacher stands in front of the class, they normally have 20 to 30 individual students with a variety of learning strengths and weaknesses. By preparing your child to take the lessons given to them in class and modify them in a way that will allow them to learn best, you give them the tools to meet any teacher's approach and succeed with them.

This is why the question we brought up earlier

becomes important. As we discussed in the first chapter, an interesting and important question you should frequently ask your child is, "If your teacher taught you lessons today in the best way for you to learn, how would they have done it?" Within that question, you have implied a few expectations: that they heard what the teacher was saying and that they will know how they would remember it best. A teacher can hardly be expected to teach 25 or more children using each one's strongest learning modality. This is where a child's adaptability comes in handy. Previous discussions with them and their own understanding of their strength allow for a clear evaluation where a strong approach can be formulated.

Reinforce this regularly, and soon your child will be conscious that this is going to be their approach. Even as they sit in class, that question will be circulating in their minds preparing them for the learning process. If they are practiced in using techniques that match their learning preference, they will be constructing their own approach to the individual lessons they have even as the class progresses. Because they have a practiced approach to learning new material, they will have confidence as they sit in class. The teacher's method or the type of material becomes less important. The perception will be created that they can learn from anyone. That is a powerful perception.

Whatever method is best for your child, you should utilize it. Build the techniques early on, and allow them to become the normal established method to succeed. This becomes increasingly important as your child progresses beyond the first few grades.

As they take ownership of their own learning strength, the expectation of being able to succeed no matter the teacher's approach or the topic at hand, breeds self-esteem and confidence.

Chapter Three

BRAIN WIRING

Understanding how the brain works will allow you to better understand how your child learns and how they can progress in their lives at school and beyond.

The Mind Model

To give you a greater understanding of how the brain works, I will use the mind model created by Gerald Kein of Omni Hypnosis. Omni Hypnosis is one of the leading hypnosis schools in the world. Omni-trained hypnotists are constantly looking to expand the use of hypnosis for people's betterment.

This is not an extensive exploration of the parts of the brain but is created with the purpose of exposing how the mind works and creating a context to apply that knowledge to your child's learning.

In this model, the mind is separated into two components: the conscious and subconscious minds.

Conscious Mind

The conscious mind is **analytical**. For example:

You chose this book for a reason. You analyzed a situation and determined that this book could help your child. You either evaluated your child's current success or decided to prepare for the upcoming school years. After considering a few options, you determined you would take action to help your child improve in school or better prepare them as they begin a new year. You did this at the conscious level.

The conscious mind is also **rational**. For example:

Had this book been incredibly expensive, you would have had to rationalize the outlay of funds to buy it. You would have had to rationalize the value of your child's long-term education against the expense of this book. When things in life do not go as planned, the rational mind puts them into perspective, so that we can make it through the day. People who have difficulty rationalizing the events of the day frequently have problems that need to be addressed by trained professionals.

When a child fails to do well on an exam, the rational mind might tell them they are not as smart as other children in the class. Their conscious mind forms a simple justification to allow them to put their exam into perspective. If this happens too frequently, they begin to accept this as a fact, and that acceptance becomes the new normal. This obviously needs to be avoided.

Another aspect of the conscious mind is the **short-term working memory**. For example:

As you get up in the morning, you know what you have to do in the course of the day. You know the people you work with, as well as the route you follow to get to work. You also know skills that are necessary to do your job well. You understand coworkers' idiosyncrasies so that you can do your job efficiently while avoiding conflict. The short-term working memory allows you to get through the day more easily.

The final aspect of the conscious mind we will discuss is **willpower**. Willpower is a wonderful thing. While it certainly can start you toward achieving a task or project, it is not designed for the long-term change. Think of willpower as the first stage of a three-stage rocket. It will get you off the launch pad, but it will not get you into outer space.

Undoubtedly, you know someone who's been able to put down cigarettes for a few weeks but somehow they are drawn back to them. This is an example of the conscious mind being unable to make long-term change. Your child will not be smoking though, so how does this apply?

If your student uses strictly willpower to sit down, study or do homework, they likely will fall short. You are failing to utilize all the tools necessary to fully engage your child in the process. To truly affect your child's long-term success, you must deal with their subconscious mind.

Subconscious Mind

To create a long-term change in someone's life, you have to deal with the subconscious mind. The subconscious mind is like a supercomputer with the ability to touch, taste and hear. The subconscious mind remembers everything that's ever happened in your life.

Beyond long-term permanent memories, the subconscious mind also deals with emotions. Memories and emotions are frequently combined. An example of this is a first impression. Upon meeting someone for the first time, you may have found that you instantly liked them or disliked them. You have no idea where that emotion came from. You remember no previous interaction with them, but somehow that emotion lingers. Previous interactions or imprints in your subconscious mind brought up those feelings causing your initial reaction. The way the person spoke, looked or dressed triggered a memory of a previous experience within you, and the emotion was tied in with them. This is not an unusual experience.

Another example of how the emotions and the senses create a feeling or memory is more pleasant and accessible. Perhaps you walked into a restaurant, and the smell of a certain food brought you back to your mother, grandmother or even your father who had cooked a similar meal. Positive memories come back, and you begin to associate the feelings you had as a child with the restaurant you just entered. As you eat at the restaurant, you make another assessment of the foods' quality. Perhaps the waiter was not particularly satisfactory or the bread slightly stale. Certainly all those issues will determine if you're going back to that restaurant, but those negative feelings must override the nostalgic feelings that initially arose attached to those pleasant early memories.

When the emotions become involved, the memory gets locked in. This is instructive when a child is trying to lock in lessons in school. When emotions are highlighted, they leave a lasting impression that can be recalled more easily.

Ultimately, the subconscious mind has one overriding principle: to protect a person against all danger, real and imagined.

Another important aspect of the subconscious mind is the creation of habits. Habits are neither good nor bad; they are merely utilitarian. When you get up in the morning, you have an established pattern that allows your life to go more smoothly. Perhaps that involves letting your dog out as you're putting on the coffee. It could mean taking a shower, brushing your teeth and applying makeup. These habits allow people to go through life without having to put in as much mental effort to plan and execute their normal daily activities.

You will note that these activities started in the conscious mind but repetition moved them to the subconscious mind. This repetition creates an impression within the subconscious mind of the importance of these habits. Because the subconscious mind views them as so important, they are difficult to change.

For those of you who remember your dreams, undoubtedly you remember a time when you had a nightmare. When you awoke, your heart may have been racing, you may have been breathing heavily or you even may have been sweating. While the danger was not real, the subconscious mind prepared you for fight, flight or freeze. Your subconscious mind was protecting you.

Programming for Positive Results

You'll note in the first few chapters of this book, many things were repeated in different ways. This was intentional. By placing important information in several places and repeating it, the mind begins to give it additional import. As stated before, every event in your life leaves an impression. How large the impression it makes is determined by how it is categorized. If an event occurs once, it leaves a small impression. If another imprint occurs that reflects back to the initial event, the initial impression becomes stronger.

In the previous chapter, I discussed the idea that practice makes permanent. Repetition is an important aspect of memory. Just like the patterns you utilize as you get up in the morning moves from the conscious to the subconscious because of repetition, repeating something designed to improve your ability to learn over and over again locks it into that subconscious permanent memory.

It is frequently acknowledged that people who repeatedly drive the same long distances often forget the many miles they have covered. Soon, they realize they've driven 200 or 300 miles with little memory of the trip. Because they have driven the route so many times before, the driving becomes almost automatic and their conscious mind is not necessarily aware of it occurring. The skill and technique of driving have been reinforced so frequently that the conscious mind does not need to be fully present.

A pattern had been established that when the person drove, everything would be all right. That pattern could possibly have been interrupted if the driver had experienced an accident on a previous trip along the same route. That negative impression would remain with them and cause their conscious mind to be fully aware of the trip.

Getting a Grip on Homework

Habits and patterns are established from the very beginning, which is why the first two chapters were created and emphasized the positive feeling children should have when they begin to question and learn. If children have an established pattern of feeling negative about something, that impression will remain. This creates avoidance behaviors. This can be seen in students claiming to have no homework, coming home, and going to their rooms to play video games or running outside to play instead of doing homework. From previous experience, the student has come to believe the homework does not help. They made an evaluation, balancing the time involved against the perceived positive reward. The avoidance behavior is an answer to that calculation.

In truth, you should be excited about your child going to school and learning. You should be excited about the homework they have. The purpose of homework is to show increasing mastery of the material they have learned. Being fully engaged in the homework, or actively using their imaginations to test their learning tools against the work, should not be viewed as a chore. For those of you using this book to reframe your older children's learning experience, create the new positive view of homework as a constructive habit and continually reinforce it until it becomes the new normal.

Your child's purpose should become completing the homework as thoroughly and quickly as possible. That is the game. Checking the material is used to prevent making silly and careless mistakes. When they are done, checking should be designed to show they have taken the task seriously and to show how they are capable of modifying or changing mistakes when they occur. The emphasis on homework should never be placed on getting it correct the first time, but on learning how to catch mistakes and correct errors.

If you check your child's homework, emphasize the pride you have when they find a mistake in their work. This creates in them the expectation of the positive reward they will get when they learn from their mistakes.

This is where the use of habits comes in handy. When the expectation of doing homework and the positive feeling of accomplishing it are locked in, the momentum of doing it continues.

For parents who do not instill positive feelings

and expectations about homework within their children by the time children get to fifth or sixth grade, the response to whether they have homework is predictable. The reasons for this are pretty clear; all the previous times their children had been asked about homework or school, there had been no expectation of a thorough and interesting answer. There was no emotion or importance given to the response, so no lasting impression was made. The value of homework was minimized.

As a teacher for over 20 years, I understand that children often have too much homework. I will not advocate for more homework at any time. The idea of this chapter is to create a positive feeling for homework, so avoiding it, or simply not doing it, is no longer an option.

Getting the Most Out of School

If a child is conditioned from early on that parents are excited and happy to hear about their day, they will feed on that excitement, and a positive imprint will remain with them. The habit of feeling good when they discuss their work with their parents will go into their long-term memory and be reinforced every time it occurs.

Additionally, by having the child recall what they have learned for the day, the lessons are repeated in their mind. Eventually, the child will begin to see that they're going to be asked the same questions every day. In preparation for this, they will listen to the lessons of the day, so that they can share them more fully with their parents. The teacher's agenda may be designed around the child mastering skills for the skill's sake. The child's agenda is pleasing the parents at home.

This is actually an avoidance behavior. Your child will want to avoid the awkward feeling of not knowing what to talk about when they get home, so they will be prepared for the questions. It is important to keep these conversations pleasant, light-hearted and social so as to avoid feelings of interrogation.

The subconscious mind will reinforce for the child the need to remember those lessons fully enough to share with the parents. Because the pattern of being questioned is established, it becomes permanent.

This method can certainly be applied to older children as well. All positive and negative habits can be replaced if a new and constant effort is made. Starting at the beginning of the year allows children who are older to reset their expectations and build themselves back up for the new school year.

If children repeatedly tell themselves that they are stupid or not able to do the work, they are sabotaging their chances of success.

Self-talk

For a child to succeed in life, knowing how to practice positive self-talk is crucial. If children consistently repeat to themselves that they are smart and are able to learn easily, they are creating the neural connections necessary to allow them to succeed.

The opposite is also true. If they do fail, they reinforce their prediction, and it is repeated over and over into their subconscious mind. They may only fail at the task once, but the repetition in their mind, combined with the negative self-talk, compounds the damage done.

Self-talk does not entail creating a false sense of identity or preclude the acknowledgement that mistakes will be made and not all attempts at achieving a goal will go smoothly. For the purposes of your child's long-term growth, self-talk needs to be focused on the fact that they will learn from their experiences and not repeat the same mistakes. That is what education is about.

"He who learns must suffer, and, even in our sleep, pain that cannot forget falls drop by drop against the heart, and in our own despair, against our will, comes wisdom to us by the awful grace of God."
– Aeschylus

Aeschylus certainly could be viewed as taking learning too seriously, but preparing your child for the setbacks that will naturally arise is a sensible course of action. In truth, you are preparing your child to end the suffering they associate with learning.

That learned attitude will allow your child to develop the mechanisms to cope with the everyday bumps and bruises that life will offer and instill the ability to bounce back from these adversities. These past few chapters were designed to allow the suffering to be as minimal as possible. If children truly find learning painful, they will avoid it.

Learning Is a Game to Be Played

Mark Twain's great American novel, *Tom Sawyer*, describes an important scene that demonstrates how a shift in mindset can change the way children feel about a chore:

As a punishment, Tom is assigned the task of painting an enormous fence, and he realizes he will not have time to play on Saturday. He decides to use his friends to paint the fence for him and does this by cleverly pretending that he is having so much fun doing it. Soon they all want to be part of the fun, and they all, Tom included, end up having great fun painting together.

In this scene, it is clear to see how the entire mindset

between what was work and what was fun changed.

Should a child go to school with the mindset that they are going to discover how well and how efficiently they can learn, they could view their experiences at school as an enjoyable game to be played. The report card could become a scoreboard pointing out the areas in need of improvement. Just as the joy I took in learning about baseball was redirected to my studies of mathematics, reading, history and sociology, so too can they begin to view their experiences in school as joyful ones to be built upon.

When children see report cards as an evaluation of who they are as human beings, they cannot help but feel pressured. If, however, they go to school and view the learning experience as a game in which they must challenge themselves to determine how well they can learn and apply the information they are given, they will find joy in the activity.

The Mind Palace

Anyone searching his or her memory to find which events stand out could well discover a common theme. It is commonly acknowledged that memories most easily accessible to us tend to be associated with an emotional event. When emotions become involved, they latch onto the memory and give it greater importance.

As such, it is useful to associate an emotion or action with a memory when you want your child to learn and remember something.

It is the application of that understanding that will allow your children to more easily recall what they are taught in school.

The Mind Palace memory technique has its roots in the ancient Roman and Greek civilization. The elements involved in this technique are relatively simple:

Think of a memory as an overcoat that must be hung on the hook. You know where the hook is — that has a long-established place in your memory. Because you're easily capable of returning to that hook, anything you know you have left there will be easily found.

In an earlier chapter, you read the story to your child about entering the kitchen going to the refrigerator and taking out a lemon. As you read that story, a particular kitchen came to your mind. It is likely the kitchen is your own or one you're familiar with already. As you think back on that story, you can see how memories are associated with the familiar.

Things become familiar because they have been repeated or given additional prominence. The additional prominence has frequently been created by an event that is linked with emotion. One example of this is what occurs before an accident. You're driving along focusing on arriving at your destination when something happens that caused an accident. That moment, because of the feeling of danger and uncertainty, becomes etched in your memory.

The emotion necessary to lock in a memory does not necessarily have to be unpleasant. Parents frequently remember the first time they held their child, when their child first began walking or when they said their first word. Because the subconscious mind locks into the emotion involved, it makes the memory available.

The reason the technique is called the Palace of Memories is because the memories are connected to a place or peg that is locked in to the person's permanent recall process. The standard memory palace for anyone starting out is a family home.

The Memory Palace was coined when Simonides

of Ceos left a banquet hall that subsequently collapsed. Remembering where all the people in the hall were seated, Simonides went with their families and used those memories to locate the position of those who were in the hall. This is the idea of the loci or location. Using well-established locations that are familiar in the memory, you can place objects there in interesting provocative manners so they can be more easily recalled.

Standard Memory Palace

Imagine your own home as you walk in the front door. You create a pattern as you walk through your entrance. Perhaps there is a table or a chair as soon as you enter. There could be a stairway nearby, but as you walk through your house there are different places or pegs that have been there for a good period of time. Each one of these familiar places can be used as a memory hook. Your child has made his or her particular room the perfect spot for a palace. They may have a light switch, a table, a lamp, a chair, a dresser and, of course, their bed to put things on. Were they to stray from their room, there may well be hundreds of different locations in the house that they can lock onto and identify with.

To build and strengthen your child's memory, try this game with them.

The Linking Game

Make a list of any sort with strange and odd objects for your child to remember. Have them go through their bedroom and point out the places/things within the room that are memorable to them. From there, tell them to number the objects in the room from one to ten. For example: the door could be the first thing, the light switch, the second, the lamp the third. In their minds, they will associate the order of objects in the room with their trip through the room. To give you a demonstration, let me create two lists.

The strange object list	10 hooks in the bedroom
1. octopus	1. doorknob
2. shoes	2. light switch
3. car	3. desk
4. paperclip	4. lamp
5. computer	5. toy chest
6. witch	6. bookshelf
7. fence	7. dresser drawer
8. grandfather	8. closet
9. movie	9. coat rack
10. tree	10. bed

The first list is for your child to remember. The second list is their room and the objects they would see as they walked through it.

To get them to remember the objects, link the two corresponding objects across the lists.

For example:

Ask them to think of the door being made of an octopus. The emotions thoughts and ideas about the octopus should be as vivid as they can make them — squishy, ugly and wet.

Link the second pair of objects by suggesting that when trying to turn on the light switch, their hand goes into an old, ugly, muddy golf shoe that stinks from never being cleaned.

Link the third set of objects by telling them to picture the lamp in the shape of a car that is spewing gas fumes.

Continue in this way and encourage your child to be creative and imaginative.

This game represents a standard example of a memory palace. There were ten clearly defined spaces in your child's established long-term memory of the objects in their room. The objects are put in the order that the 10 spaces or hooks had been established. Because we naturally try to categorize the place of things in the appropriate spots, the way the story was told makes it odd. Because it is odd and doesn't fit logically, the memory becomes stronger. Additionally, touch, smell, hearing and other senses are brought in to magnify the memory.

By practicing memory games like this with your child, they began to supercharge their imaginations and abilities to remember things.

The game below is useful to play competitively with your older children.

Memory Game

Use your memory technique to memorize all the presidents of the United States in order. Access the information online or research it in an encyclopedia.

Each of you print the list or write it down, then look at it for two minutes, examining it and realizing that in 20 minutes, you will have the list memorized.

Relax and remind yourself that you will do this easily and quickly.

Spend 20 minutes imagining the most outrageous, funny pictures of one president after another. You are just getting their names — don't worry about what they really look like. Use a memory palace or quick association to lock them in.

Once the 20 minutes are up, put the list aside, take a

deep, relaxing breath and let the images flow from one to the next. As these memories move from one to the other, both of you write the names down. This is a mental exercise, so you cannot fail. This will tell you how far you have progressed in developing your skill. Giving your child an opportunity to meet you on an even playing field will be fun for them and ingrain the technique, as well.

Memory Game 2

In this game, you'll use a visual link to remember facts. Here are a few more examples of using your creative imaginations to lock in information.

Eugene O'Neill was a playwright in the early 1900s who won five Pulitzer Prizes. In 1936, he won the Nobel Prize in Literature. This is an award even Mark Twain never won.

To remember these facts do the following: Concentrate on remembering the name *Eugene O'Neill*. Do this by first visualizing him in as silly a way as possible — a bright blue dog with an ostrich neck and big purple eyes.

Now think of a giant letter *U* putting on a pair of jeans —this should lead you to *Eugene*. As *Eugene* puts on his jeans, he falls through a giant letter *O* and falls on his knees and is now *kneeling* — *O'Neill*.

The rest of the information could be connected in a similar way as you practiced with the Memory Palace.

The stranger and more active a story, the easier it is to remember. This technique is like any other — the more you practice it, the easier it is to come up with the pictures, ideas and hooks to attach the material to.

By having your child take the lists of information they need to learn and using their imaginations to create a vivid picture or story that deals with that information, they will become more skilled at recall.

Each day, as more lessons come their way, they have the opportunity to use this fun and interesting technique to master the new material. Have them make the images vivid, strange or funny, as they'll be easier to remember. Encourage them to use colors, emotions and the senses of sound, taste and touch to aid them.

The example I used was deliberately something you probably aren't interested in. Your child will have a background with much of the information they are going to learn, so their own memories and ideas will make vivid and more memorable stories.

If they have friends who have the same name as characters in stories they read, they can put them into the stories doing the actions in funny, interesting or ridiculous ways. That is a natural hook for them.

As they get older and begin studying subjects like mathematics and science, they might need to know who Gregor Mendel is. Well, he deals with genes. They could imagine a man mending blue jeans. When you see the name Mendel, you will remember genes.

In math, they might need to remember the following formula:

$$x = \frac{-b \pm \sqrt{b^2 - 4ac}}{2a}$$

How would you use this technique to remember this formula?

You know that the formula is to equal x. -b is a b that is negative, so you have an angry bee (a positive b would be happy). This b is on the second floor of a house.

This negative bee sees a plus and a minus sign fighting to the death. As they fight, they hit the wall and a giant square root of a shelter comes out.

Underneath this shelter, you see a bee that is square shaped (b2). Four separate air conditioners pull (-) at the four corners of the bee (-4ac). They are all under the square root shelter.

They hear a noise from underneath. Two giant ants (2a) are pushing against the ceiling trying to get at the second floor, but they cannot.

Many of you know this formula, but those who are learning it for the first time could use this method to lock it in and learn it in less than three minutes if they use their imaginations.

Students can apply this technique to anything they want to learn. They only have to practice. As they come home with more things to memorize, they can practice using this technique until it becomes normal and ingrained for them. Their creative training will allow them to more quickly invent memorable stories to prepare them for quizzes and tests,

Chapter Four

WHERE IS THE SCHOOL?

If the past three chapters have done nothing else, they should have established that children learn no matter where they are. By going over the techniques discussed, your children will have discovered this clearly. They will discover that learning is a natural and frequently fun activity.

Their previous life experiences have all been designed to instill in them an open mind to receive and remember information more easily. This does not preclude them from having certain subjects that are more difficult than others. However, the foundation for them to succeed in the formalized academic setting of the school will have been established.

As was discussed in earlier chapters, creating a positive environment for your children as they go to school for the first time is a vital ingredient to their eventual success. The formal education they enter into is merely an extension of the life they have already led. Education and viewing the world as a place to learn and extend their knowledge is the normal course of things.

School surrounds your children as they experience life. The lessons they learned in their early lives have prepared them for an education no matter where it occurs.

Become Familiar with Their Environment

We all have places where we feel more comfortable. Many people will retreat to their bedroom to go online, read quietly, study, text their friends or even catch a quick nap before dinner. The room itself is actually no more than wood, brick or wallpaper with furniture, yet you have made it something else: a haven from the rest of the world.

When your child walks into a classroom, do they find it strange or off-putting? When I prepared for my SATs, one of the first things I did was arrive early so I could see which room I would be taking my test in. I went in early and looked at the entire room. Soon, I knew the entire place and made a firm decision that I would feel comfortable there. I looked at the writing on the board and decided that I liked the handwriting. I saw the pictures on the walls and thought about how interesting they were. Within my mind, I decided I was going to like the place and I would succeed there. As I sat down in my assigned space, I felt comfortable and capable of doing great work. I was focused and relaxed, and I knew no matter what questions appeared on the test, I would be able to answer them easily and correctly. I knew that if I finished early, I could go back and examine the previous questions to ensure I did not make any silly mistakes.

The room became part of my process. I knew I would do well there.

When your child goes to school, have them go to the room and become comfortable there. In their early years, the school will focus on social skills and basic learning. They must realize it doesn't matter where they sit or whether they are away from their friends — their job is to focus on the material at hand. Your child's purpose is to use their imagination to imbue that room with the qualities that will allow them to gain knowledge at an incredible rate. They are creating that room to be a comfortable, safe place where learning comes easily. If they build the expectation for success, it is far more likely to come. As children, they will have a loose focus that allows for being distracted occasionally.

That classroom is not very different from their bedroom. It may not have a bed, the same type of desk or a computer, but it is made of wood or brick, or has walls covered in wallpaper, and they will learn well there.

Since the classroom is new, your child can use it as a location, a loci to place objects. They can place the memories they need to recall on tests in the different locations in the room. This is just another way of using their imagination to make learning fun and easier.

If you are reading this book for older students who need to refocus their efforts on becoming a life-long learner, their perception of the classroom may need to be modified. After years of seeing their classroom as a place of difficulty, they can practice taking the time to imagine it being a positive place of learning. Through repetition, the negative perception of the classroom can be changed. Rest assured that with frequent repetition, the habit of seeing their classroom positively will take place.

Encourage Your Child to Be a Noticer

What the heck does that mean? Be a noticer?

Throughout our lives, we notice millions of things without realizing it. You might see a dog out of the corner of your eye; if you like dogs, you might go over to pet it, or you might move to the other side of the road if you don't. When meeting up with a friend, you might instantly know something is wrong. This does not mean you have psychic ability or you can read people's minds, but you have developed a rapport or relationship with this friend that allows you to see more than is evident to others.

You do not think about noticing things; it just comes naturally. Some people notice things all the time and become distracted. Some say these people lack focus, but harnessing the ability to notice in the right direction can be a major asset. By your child using their natural ability to notice things, they will also start to accumulate knowledge more easily.

For older students who are looking to improve, this can be a valuable lesson. As they enter class, they may notice their teacher has written something on the board. Of course, they will write that down in their notebooks as soon as they sit down. They may want to take notice of what the teacher is emphasizing for the day. What is it that the teacher wants them to learn? They may not know, but may ask themselves to guess what their teacher wants. It is helpful to have them write down what they think the lesson for the day will be. This should be discussed with them before they go to school. The great news is they do not need to be right. This is the preparation for accepting the lessons to come.

This is a game they can play to determine whether or not they are being observant and capable of putting things together before class begins. They are beginning to map the information that may go into their incredible developing memory. The power to notice as they sit down is best used on the material their teacher gives them, or the text that has been assigned. Believe me, anyone can become distracted by the things around them. So the challenge in this game is to see how much they can notice about the things that will enable them to learn better.

As the teacher goes to the board, they should take note of whether they are right-handed or left-handed. Does the teacher use cursive or block lettering? Is the teacher's handwriting neat?

As the child takes notes, have them draw a square in the top right-hand side of their page. Tell them to identify a word or phrase that the teacher frequently uses. Because I was raised in the north and spent a good deal of time in Canada, my students noticed that I said "eh" at the end of many sentences. Because I taught them to pay attention, they frequently noticed that I said it seven or eight times throughout the course of a class.

At the end of the period, my students would compare their numbers. Yes, sometimes they would disagree, but while they were focused on listening for that phrase or sound, they were also focused on taking thorough notes. Of course, they were listening for the important class material, but because they had a relaxed focus on another subject, the students seemed to receive the information more easily.

Instruct your student to do this with their notes. Have them mark at the top of their paper the odd or unusual things their teacher or fellow students do. Tell them that every time one of these odd occurrences happens, it is a reminder to easily focus on the course material being taught.

Each teacher will teach differently; they all have small, individual quirks in the way they talk, the way they move or the method they use to teach. Taking the time to see exactly how the teacher works will also focus students on the material to be learned.

As they return home at the end of the day, question them as to what they noticed about their teacher and friends. While they may point out the normal everyday idiosyncrasies of their teacher and friends, they are using this to sharpen their ability to focus.

This technique can apply to math as well. They can practice this technique as you go on a car trip. Do the license plate numbers add up to anything? Can they be divided by another number without a remainder? As you do this, you will begin to train your brain to do more and more. Think of these exercises as mental calisthenics.

Reading for Understanding

Much of this guide has been designed to set up your children for success. This section is designed for your older students who have followed the memory sections and increased their ability to remember, but are slightly deficient in their reading ability. They may not have gone through the early set up for education the first few chapters covered, but they must not feel that they cannot improve their reading skills.

After practicing training the brain to remember things, children have undoubtedly become more proficient at listening and taking quicker notes. This is the core of reading, as well.

As they look at the page, the words your child reads should begin to form pictures and vivid images in their mind. This technique allows them to remember story and plotlines more easily. By using their improved imagination and memory tools, they can activate their minds to read faster while accessing more of the material.

They have the tools to read more easily. They may find words that do not make perfect sense or seem out of place, but as they go along, they will be able to place them where they need to be. All communication is context. As they take what they understand and build upon it, the more difficult material will find a context that allows it to fit in, and their understanding of the more complex passages will improve.

As children read, they are developing the background for all the information that follows. Most stories have a beginning, middle and an end. The beginning introduces them to the characters, problems, conflicts and themes. From this, they put the information together for the rest of the story. The beginning and all the introductory information is a leg for the book's table.

As they lock down the characters, they should make them as whole as they can. They should be imagining their hair color, eye color and height in as much detail as they can. As they progress through the book, they use this image as the characters go through their actions or think about what they are doing. As a parent, you have been cultivating their imagination for a long time now so that it can be used. The more vivid the actions in their imagination, the more easily they will be able to access them when needed.

Once again, they should not read the text and imagine the story exactly as it is written. Make it more bizarre and memorable. The more they put into it, the better. Their job as they go through a text is to make it as enjoyable as possible so their mind will be able to remember it.

Step One

As they sit down with the book in front of them, they should lock down that they will love reading it. If they allow the thought of not enjoying the book to creep in, they will make reading a chore. They have become practiced at using their imagination and memory in a powerful way. Apply it to this task and watch how quickly they can read and understand.

Step Two

As they go through the book, they should not be afraid to imagine the characters as people they know, or as their friends. They have an interest in what their friends do, so consider that interest to be their reading hook for remembering. They can take hold of their friend's actions within the text and watch what progresses. Clearly, they know this character is not their real friend, but their imagination will focus more easily and intently on the action with the help of the hook. They have given their mind a reason to care about the novel, book, poem or short story.

Step Three

One of my favorite books is Illusions, by Richard Bach. A favorite quote from the book says, "Argue for your limitations and they are yours." Do not limit their ability to read by allowing them to believe they are slow readers. If they have a reading challenge and are working with a teacher, their job is to make her feel like she is the greatest teacher in the world. They must go in with the attitude that they will take in everything she teaches them, take good notes and utilize them fully. Each day they will be increasing both their reading speed and their understanding. Apply their easy focus techniques from the first few chapters to all their classes.

Remember when we discussed how they could look at a friend and know if he'd had a hard day and how he felt? Well, reading a book is similar. They are taking black ink on a white sheet of paper and giving it meaning. The author intended for them to have some understanding of the material and their teacher will guide them as well, but it is they who are doing the reading. They should use the techniques you have shared with them, so they can enjoy the power and ability that they have worked to improve.

Step Four

Perhaps the most vital thing they can do to become a better reader is to read often. They have books that are required for school, but encourage them to read everything they can. As I mentioned earlier, feed their passion. If they love sports, encourage them to read as many sports books as they can.

When they read, expect them to understand the material. Have them take a few moments before reading to close their eyes; think about what they think will be in the story. It's okay if they aren't right: if they make it vivid and it is wrong, their mind will remember the correction clearly, and they will still have the material there.

Step Five

Remember that they are capable, and no one can make them think otherwise without their consent. They should not allow other people's limited beliefs to stop them. If someone says something negative about their ability to read, learn or do anything, they can reject that comment. If they give them information or a lesson to help them on their way, they can accept the positive input and reject the negativity.

Practice

They should take the notes or questions their teacher gives them before they read their book and read them thoroughly before reading the text. These questions will guide them to what is important within the text. In their mind, they should map out what they think will happen based on their questions and notes. If they are given a short story to read and there are questions listed at the back of the text, they should use them to focus their direction. If there is no information provided beforehand, they can allow their mind to be clear and let the words paint the blank canvas. All the previous work you have done with them has trained them to use their imagination as fully as they can.

You can go over this section of the chapter with them or even copy the relevant sections for their use.

Reading Log

Whatever they read, keeping a log with general information on characters, plots and storylines is a great idea. From these logs they can compare and contrast different writing styles and create contexts for their further reading.

Writing by Making Connections

As your children write, think or speak, they are communicating. As they memorize material for class, they are communicating with their mind, telling it what is expected and what it will do. If they have been practicing these techniques in everyday life, their mind is beginning to realize that going along and doing the work is easier than fighting it all the time.

They are retraining their brain to think and make connections. One of the principles we discussed is the fact that they have to make hooks and memory pegs that relate to their lives. These pegs could have been created from childhood friends, from previous experiences, from a television show they saw or from an event that marked a special occasion in their life. Whatever they have used to create those memory pegs has shown them something: They can make connections.

How does this apply to their writing? Well, when their teachers ask them to write on a topic, they attempt to be correct, to do it right or to impress them with their knowledge. These are lofty goals, but if they have ever had the dreaded writer's block, they have frozen when they attempted to do the assignment or put the paper together.

Think of their pegs as places to put information. Their paper is the closet that holds the information they must put together. With any luck, they have a good foundation in grammar that will serve them well. If not, they can use the techniques they have learned to remember the rules of proper grammar. Grammar is important, but it is the content of the paper that stymies most people.

They must put forward certain information in a paper that their teacher and their audience need to know. However, simply putting in bits of information is not sufficient to get the best grade. Context is the biggest key. Context tells them why something is important.

They have created context for their assignments/notes to be remembered. When they write their papers, they are doing the same thing; they are taking the information and putting it into an appropriate context for their teacher. They are explaining why the information is important to understand. They have used their minds to make the information they have learned fresh and interesting. They should use their minds to find creative ways of utilizing that information in new and interesting ways.

Have they ever seen a movie they particularly liked? Well, there was a structure to that movie. As they write, they become the director, putting all the scenes (ideas) together. When they are done, they will have put this paper together in a way that is interesting, covers all the issues their teacher wants discussed and is easy to follow. If you have shared the important information on note-taking, they will know what their teacher wants in terms of formatting or content.

As they continue to read, they may find sentences or ideas they particularly like. Encourage them to use those ideas when doing their own writing. Earlier in this book, I quoted one of my favorite books to get across the point that people limit themselves. When I used the quote, I cited the book and its author. They have to give credit for ideas that are not their own, but using other people's ideas correctly shows a higher level of writing mastery.

Before beginning major standardized writing assignments in school, I would go over the plotlines of seven or eight different movies. Each movie had a slightly different theme, but by knowing them, I could take the question that was asked and apply it to the theme or idea of the movie. I used the movie's structure and placed the idea of the question against it. I related my ideas for the paper to the theme of the movie.

If your child has kept a reading log, they have other books, short stories or novels they can compare and contrast their fresh reading to. Those readings can be used in the same way as the movies we discussed.

This technique will give the paper a regulated structure and a context for the answer. This technique could put them far ahead of most writers on standardized essays. The movie gives them useful pegs where they can put the ideas and information they want to get across. This makes the paper memorable and interesting. Having been a teacher for more than 20 years, I cannot tell you the number of times a paper that had a few errors was redeemed, because it was interesting and well-constructed.

Here is a quick tip for them to remember as they write. Stories work better than dry factual writing. They have to tie the story back to their answer, but it is far better for someone who is grading a paper to be reading material that is not dry and boring. This does not mean they should avoid using all the knowledge they have, or that they should fail to answer the question fully, but they can do so in an interesting way.

Think of their previous knowledge of other books, movies, stories and their own life as the hooks they use to pull their writing together.

The following is a list of foundational writing tips:
- Each paragraph should support one idea.
- If they can say something clearly in seven words, do not use 25.
- Each paragraph should have its own beginning, middle and end.
- Vary the sentence structure. This means they should start some sentences with prepositional phrases, among other ways.

Assignment One

Have your child write out the plotline for five movies, televisions shows, novels, short stories or plays they know very well. Include the characters and the themes or ideas they seem to support.

Each plotline should have different themes or ideas so they can apply them to different situations.

They may never use these, but even if they do not, they will have a better idea of how to structure their writing.

IN CONCLUSION...

One of my favorite movies is *A League of Their Own*. This film is about a group of women who overcome stereotypes, disproving people who do not believe they will achieve great things. They become competitive baseball players in a women's league, and they play very well, even though it is challenging.

At one point during the film, one of the women finally complains that what they're doing is hard. The manager of the team essentially says that what makes it great is the fact that it is hard. If, during your life, you never challenge yourself to be better, you cannot grow.

You are your child's coach. Hopefully, you have read through this text and discovered ideas and tools they could implement to make their time in and out of school more enjoyable.

Learning does not need to be hard. The first few chapters were designed primarily for your younger children to create a receptive environment for learning. The emphasis on positive reinforcement is something that should go without saying. We run towards what we love and away from what we fear. If we love what we do, we continue doing it. Creating that positive, active environment lays the foundations for them to enjoy learning and questioning. As the habit of enjoyable learning and questioning becomes ingrained from the beginning, it will stand them in good stead throughout the rest of their lives.

As they learn to adapt and perceive the world as a place of opportunity, they set in place the patterns of learning in a natural and enjoyable way. I want to emphasize again that too much television must be avoided during the early years. Education is based upon context. Television creates its own context and that is hard to overcome. There are shows like Sesame Street, the Electric Company and, from when I was a child, Mr. Rogers, that honor the questioning of the world around you, but most television does not.

The chapters on building a better memory are best taught at an early age, so young children can use their unbridled imaginations to apply to their memory games. It is instructive to remember that young children have not had their love of learning taken away. They are sponges as they start out, which can be a curse or a blessing. You must be careful to fortify the positive things around them, while also preparing them to see the negative things in life as valuable lessons to be learned and do so without holding onto the negativity.

The chapters that followed brought your child to the school itself. Taking the time to make the school a familiar and comfortable ground is vital. If they see school as a place of learning and comfort, they will allow their natural inquisitive nature to take hold. If they become tense or distracted, the ability to learn gets hampered.

By avoiding an emphasis on a letter grade, you relieve your child of the stress that comes from over-concentration on assessments. Assessments are not learning. If your child focuses on taking the information given and being able to use it actively, they create the foundation for future learning. Excellent grades will come organically from that.

As they progress in school, a few sections were devoted to relaxing their focus so they could condition themselves to learn from their teachers. Even students who have attention problems can use the technique of splitting their focus between what their teachers are doing and the lesson at hand. If they condition themselves to be more observant about the things around them, in and outside of class, their minds will be sharpened and ready for the task of studying.

By engaging with them about their day from the beginning as they come from school, you create a normalcy and expectation that can be carried on through all their school years. The questions do not come from a concern about falling grades that need to be addressed, but from a genuine and honest interest in how their lives are progressing. This becomes an element of communication that is important in any family dynamic.

The most important questions educate the listener. They tell the person answering it which direction their thoughts should move toward. They create expectation and lead to the desire to find more answers.

The final few chapters dealt with reading and writing improvement. These two topics go hand in hand. As a child reads, they organically learn style and formatting from the authors they study. When they keep reading logs about the novels, plays and short stories they have completed, they create models they can compare their future reading and writing against.

The greatest lesson people can learn is how to teach themselves. By keeping that tenant in mind, your child will be able to adapt, learn and profit from any teacher regardless of the approach that teacher is taking.

Create and enable the tools your child already has to learn so they can prosper. Their ability to learn and apply that knowledge is already present; you are just allowing them to let it loose.

Timothy M. Horn, BCH, CI
Hypnoconsult, LLC
Feel free to contact me with any questions at
Tim@Hypnoconsult.com

STROMBOLI'S DAD'S ACKNOWLEDGEMENTS

Janet Gunn
Stromboli
Manuela Paraiso
Tim Erickson
Patty Erickson
Tom Horn
Kevin Horn
Dante
Jeff Ferrio
Katie Hackett
Max Evry
Nancy Ayanna Wyatt
Mac Cardone
Jason Linett
Tara Bejai
Katherine Gotthardt

Mary Black
Nancy Clifford Hervey
Glennie Rodford
Tom Siesmen
Ruth Taylor
Jona Blocker
Roger Kenvin
Ed Gassek
Genie Ryan
Kathy Hess
Patricia Kliewer
Joseph Dudziak
Steven Thompson
Lloyd Curtis
Borazon the Radish
SBN of Gainesville, VA

ABOUT THE AUTHOR

Timothy Horn has an impish sense of humor that once had him running a radish against two human candidates for the Prince William County Board of Supervisors in Virginia. Borazon the Radish did get eight write-in votes, much to the astonishment the County Election Board.

Tim has applied his slightly skewed point of view in many of his exploits in life. He lives by Victor Borg's maxim that the shortest distance between two people is a good laugh. With degrees in English and theatre, he combines his love of language with the creative arts to make positive changes in children's lives.

While always a good student in terms of grades, it was not until later in his life Tim began to discover the power of the human mind. Using hypnosis to overcome panic attacks, he began to explore the full range of the conscious and subconscious mind and discovered way to tear away the barriers in people's lives.

Now an internationally recognized hypnotist and speaker, Tim teaches two to three basic and advanced hypnosis classes every year. Additionally, he teaches a program called The Success Magnet, combining several techniques to allow people to identify and take action to achieve greater success and happiness in life.

To learn more about Tim's seminars and programs, visit www.Hypnoconsult.com or email Tim@hypnoconsult.com.

Made in the USA
Lexington, KY
21 November 2019